W9-ASB-847

CONTENTS

LAKE CLASSICS

*Great British and Irish
Short Stories I*

WITHDRAWN

Thomas
HARDY

Stories retold by Joanne Suter
Illustrated by James McConnell

LAKE EDUCATION
Belmont, California

LAKE CLASSICS

Great American Short Stories I

Washington Irving, Nathaniel Hawthorne, Mark Twain, Bret Harte, Edgar Allan Poe, Kate Chopin, Willa Cather, Sarah Orne Jewett, Sherwood Anderson, Charles W. Chesnutt

Great American Short Stories II

Herman Melville, Stephen Crane, Ambrose Bierce, Jack London, Edith Wharton, Charlotte Perkins Gilman, Frank R. Stockton, Hamlin Garland, O. Henry, Richard Harding Davis

Great British and Irish Short Stories I

Arthur Conan Doyle, Saki (H. H. Munro), Rudyard Kipling, Katherine Mansfield, Thomas Hardy, E. M. Forster, Robert Louis Stevenson, H. G. Wells, John Galsworthy, James Joyce

Great Short Stories from Around the World I

Guy de Maupassant, Anton Chekhov, Leo Tolstoy, Selma Lagerlöf, Alphonse Daudet, Mori Ogwai, Leopoldo Alas, Rabindranath Tagore, Fyodor Dostoevsky, Honoré de Balzac

Cover and Text Designer: Diann Abbott

Library of Congress Catalog Number: 94-075355
ISBN 1-56103-030-9
Printed in the United States of America
1 9 8 7 6 5 4 3 2

❧ Lake Classic Short Stories ❧

> *"The universe is made of stories, not atoms."*
> —Muriel Rukeyser

> *"The story's about you."*
> —Horace

Everyone loves a good story. It is hard to think of a friendlier introduction to classic literature. For one thing, short stories are *short*—quick to get into and easy to finish. Of all the literary forms, the short story is the least intimidating and the most approachable.

Great literature is an important part of our human heritage. In the belief that this heritage belongs to everyone, *Lake Classic Short Stories* are adapted for today's readers. Lengthy sentences and paragraphs are shortened. Archaic words are replaced. Modern punctuation and spellings are used. Many of the longer stories are abridged. In all the stories, painstaking care has been taken to preserve the author's unique voice.

Lake Classic Short Stories have something for everyone. The hundreds of stories in the collection cover a broad terrain of themes, story types, and styles. Literary merit was a deciding factor in story selection. But no story was included unless it was as enjoyable as it was instructive. And special priority was given to stories that shine light on the human condition.

Each book in the *Lake Classic Short Stories* is devoted to the work of a single author. Little-known stories of merit are included with famous old favorites. Taken as a whole, the collected authors and stories make up a rich and diverse sampler of the story-teller's art.

Lake Classic Short Stories guarantee a great reading experience. Readers who look for common interests, concerns, and experiences are sure to find them. Readers who bring their own gifts of perception and appreciation to the stories will be doubly rewarded.

❦ Thomas Hardy ❧
(1840–1928)

About the Author

Thomas Hardy was born in the county of Dorset, England. He was trained as an architect and worked in that profession for some years. But he eventually turned to writing as a more satisfying way to express himself. His first success as a writer came in 1893 with the novel *A Pair of Blue Eyes*.

During the next 24 years, Hardy wrote 11 novels. After that he turned almost entirely to poetry. The versatile Hardy once described himself as "an author of prose for 25 years and of verse for 28 years."

Among his best-known novels are *Tess of the D'Urbervilles*, *Jude the Obscure*, *Far from the Madding Crowd*, *The Mayor of Casterbridge*, and *The Return of the Native*.

Hardy's writing was realistic. Most of his characters were ordinary men and women living simple lives. To add to the realism, he set his stories in the area he knew best—his own county of Dorset. In his fiction he calls this area by its old name, *Wessex*. By focusing on everyday struggles, he honored the common and universal experiences of human life.

Many of Hardy's characters lose their battles against powerful social forces. But they show strength and endurance in the struggle. In this way, they demonstrate a kind of heroism.

Hardy often claimed that he was a "meliorist"—one who believes that the world can be made better by human effort.

If you enjoy intense, realistic stories about the trials of ordinary people, you'll like Thomas Hardy.

The Three Strangers

Do you put much stock in coincidence? When this story begins, it's a rainy night on the downs. One by one, three travelers come knocking at the same cottage door. Have all of them lost their way? Why do they seem to know each other?

Out of the night, the traveler appeared on the doormat.

The Three Strangers

 $\mathcal{S}$ ome of the farming country in England has changed little with the passing of time. This land rolls along in gentle hills called *downs*. It is high, grassy, and treeless. The downs cover a large area of certain counties in the south and southwest. They are home to herds of sheep. Any sign of human life there usually takes the form of a lonely shepherd's cottage.

Some 50 years ago, just such a lonely cottage stood on such a down. Possibly it is still standing there now. The spot was really not more than five miles from a town. But five miles of rough hills was a long way indeed. And the long seasons of snow and rain also separated the cottage from the rest of the world.

Usually some clump of trees or row of bushes shelters a house. But Higher Crowstairs, as this house was called, stood in the open. No doubt it was placed there because of the crossing of two footpaths nearby. These paths may have crossed just so for a good five hundred years.

The house was open to the weather on all sides. Indeed, the wind up there blew strong when it did blow, and the rain beat hard whenever it fell. But the winter weather was not so bad on the downs as those who lived on low ground thought it was.

The ice and frosts on the downs were not so deadly as in the hollows. A shepherd and his family lived in the cottage. They said they were less bothered by colds and coughs than when they had lived in a neighboring valley.

The night of March 28, 182— was one of those cold, nasty nights. The rain beat against the hills. Sheep and outdoor animals that had no shelter stood with their back ends to the wind. The tails of little birds trying to sleep on some bare bush were blown inside-out like umbrellas. The cottage was stained with wet. Its shutters flapped against the wall.

Yet there was no call to feel sorry for the shepherd and his family. For he was a cheerful fellow. And tonight was giving a party to celebrate the birth and christening of his second girl.

The guests had arrived before the rain began to fall. Now it was eight o'clock and they were all gathered in the main room. It was as cozy and comfortable a place as could be wished for in such weather. The room was lighted by half-a-dozen candles. These were set in beautiful candlesticks that were never used except for holidays. These lights were placed about the room. Two of them glowed on the chimney-piece, which always meant a party. A fire blazed on the hearth.

About 20 people were gathered here. The women wore bright-colored gowns and sat in chairs along the wall. Girls, shy and not shy, filled the window-bench. Among the men were Charley Jake, the hedge-cutter, and Elijah New, the parish clerk. John Pitcher was also there. He was a neighboring dairyman, and the shepherd's father-in-law. A man of 50 or more moved anxiously from spot to spot. He had just become engaged. Now he was following his beloved wherever she went.

Everyone was having a good time. These people knew each other well and were comfortable with each other. They were not the kind who cared about moving up the social ladder.

Shepherd Fennel had married well. As

a dairyman's daughter, his wife had brought some money to the marriage. But this money was carefully kept aside to take care of family needs. She closely watched every penny. She had given some long thought to this gathering.

At first, she had considered a sit-still party—where talk was the main fun. But she worried that the lack of movement might lead the men to drink a great deal. They might drink her house dry. A dancing-party was another idea. But this had its dangers, too. Dancing makes the guests hungry—which is hard on the pantry. So Shepherdess Fennel decided to mix short dances with short periods of talk and singing. But this was her plan alone. The shepherd himself was in the mood to share everything he had with his guests.

The fiddler was a boy of those parts, around 12 years of age. He played some wonderful jigs and reels. Elijah New, the parish-clerk, played along on a horn. At seven came the tweedle-dee of music, and the dancing had begun. Mrs. Fennel quietly told the players what to do. On no account, she said, should they let the dance last longer than a quarter of an hour.

But Elijah and the boy got lost in their music. They quite forgot her words. Mrs. Fennel saw that her guests were dancing on and on. She knew they were surely growing hungry. Crossing over the room, she touched the fiddler's arm. Then she put her hand over the end of the horn. But they took no notice. Afraid that she might be thought a poor hostess, she sat down, helpless. And so the dancing went on. At last the hand of the old clock had circled more than an hour.

While all was cheerful within Fennel's cottage, something quite different was happening in the gloomy night without. As Mrs. Fennel worried about the dance, a human figure was climbing the hill to Higher Crowstairs. Coming from the town, this person moved steadily through the rain without stopping. He followed the little path that passed by the shepherd's cottage.

It was nearly the time of full moon. The sky, of course, was lined with dripping clouds. But even at that, there was moonlight. The sad, pale light showed the lonely traveler to be a man. His walk suggested that he was not young, but also not old. Perhaps he was about 40 years of age. Because he was very thin, he appeared tall. But in fact, he was not more than about five-feet-eight.

The man's steps were regular but careful. His coat was not black. But there was something about him that suggested that he should be dressed in black. He wore peasants' clothing of thick cotton, and his boots were heavy. Yet his careful steps showed that he was not at home on the muddy downs.

The rain started coming down harder when he arrived at the shepherd's cottage. He stopped and looked about for cover. The shine of moonlight on a small shed caught the traveler's eye. He turned off the path. Finding the shed empty, he stood under its roof.

The boom of the horn and the sound of the fiddle reached the spot where he stood. He looked toward the nearby house. The notes were mixed with the beat of rain on the cabbage-leaves in the garden. The music danced around the eight or ten beehives near the path.

Then the music stopped and the house was quiet. The silence seemed to shake the lone traveler into action. He left the shed and walked up the path to the house. He lifted his hand to knock, but then stopped and stared at the closed door. The dark wood showed nothing. Yet it seemed he was trying to look through the door—wondering what sort of house this might be.

He turned and looked around. Not a person was anywhere in sight. The garden path stretched downward from his feet. It was shining in the pale moonlight like the track of a snail. Far away in the valley, a faint whiteness showed that the rivers were high. Beyond all this winked a few lamplights in the town from which he had appeared to come. He knocked at the door.

Within, the dancing had ended and the people were talking. The hedge-cutter was trying to get everyone to sing. But nobody seemed interested, and the knock came as a welcome excuse.

"Walk in!" said the shepherd quickly.

The latch clicked upward. Out of the night, the traveler appeared upon the door mat. The shepherd got up and turned to look at him. In the candlelight, he could see that the stranger had dark skin and was quite good-looking. His hat was pulled low but did not hide his eyes. They were large, open, and steady. In a flash, his eyes moved around the room. The man seemed pleased with what he saw. He took the hat off of his shaggy head. Then he said in a rich, deep voice, "The rain is heavy, friends. May I ask your leave to come in and rest a while?"

"To be sure, stranger," said the shepherd. "You have been lucky in choosing your time. Tonight we are having a party for a happy cause."

"And what may be this glad cause?" asked the stranger.

"A birth and christening," said the shepherd.

The stranger wished his host well. When invited to take a drink from the mug, he readily agreed.

"Late to be wandering about the downs, hey?" said the newly engaged man of 50.

"Late it is, as you say. I'll take a seat in the chimney-corner, if it's all right with you, ma'am. I am a little wet from the rain."

Mrs. Shepherd Fennel nodded. She made room for the self-invited newcomer.

He stretched out his legs and arms and made himself quite at home.

"Yes, they're rather worn through," he said. He had seen the eyes of the shepherd's wife fall upon his old boots. "And I'm not very well-dressed, either. I've had some rough times lately. My difficulties have forced me to pick up what I can get in the way of clothes. Before I reach home, I must find a suit better fit for working-days."

"Are you from around here?" asked Shepherdess Fennel.

"Not quite. Farther up the country."

"I thought so. And so be I. From the way you talk, I thought you might come from my neighborhood."

"But you would hardly have heard of me," he said quickly. "I'm much older than you, ma'am."

This mention of age stopped the hostess's questions.

"There is only one thing I need to make me happy," continued the newcomer.

"That is just a bit of tobacco. I'm sorry to say that I am out of it."

"I'll fill your pipe," said the shepherd.

"I must ask you to lend me a pipe, too."

"A smoker—and no pipe?"

"I have dropped it somewhere on the road."

The shepherd filled a new clay pipe. He handed it to the traveler. "Give me your tobacco box," he said. "I'll fill that up for you, too."

The man went through the motions of searching his pockets.

"Lost that, too?" said the shepherd, with some surprise.

"I am afraid so," said the man. "If you will give it to me in a piece of paper?" Lighting his pipe at the candle, he resettled himself in the corner. Then he turned his eyes on the steam that rose from his wet legs. He looked as if he wished to say no more.

Meanwhile, the rest of the guests took

little notice of the visitor. They were talking to the fiddler about music for the next dance. The matter being settled, they were about to stand up when there came another knock at the door.

At the knock, the man in the chimney-corner picked up the poker. Then he began stirring the ashes as if this were his one aim in life. For the second time, the shepherd said, "Walk in!" In a moment, another man stood upon the straw door mat. He, too, was a stranger.

This person was very different from the first. He seemed a more ordinary sort of man. There was a certain happy, man-of-the-world look about him. He was several years older than the first visitor. His hair was slightly frosted, his eyebrows thick, and his whiskers cut back from his cheeks. His face was rather full and fat—yet it was not altogether a face without power.

Now he flung back his long, dark coat.

Under his coat he wore a fine suit the color of gray ashes. Shaking the water-drops from his hat, he turned to his host. "I must ask for a few minutes' shelter, friends. If not, I shall be wet to my skin before I get to Casterbridge."

"Make yourself at home," said the shepherd. His voice was, perhaps, a bit less cheery than on the first occasion. Not that Fennel was the least bit stingy. But the room was far from large. The steamy smell of the damp visitors was not altogether pleasant for the women and girls in their bright-colored gowns.

The second visitor took off his coat. He hung his hat on a nail as if he had been invited to put it there. He sat down at the table. To give more room to the dancers, the table had been pushed closely into the chimney corner. Its edge rubbed the elbow of the man who had settled himself by the fire. Thus the two strangers were brought close together. They nodded to each other. The first stranger handed his neighbor the family cup. It was a huge, brown mug. Its rim was worn by generations of thirsty lips.

The other man raised the mug to his lips. He drank on, and on, and on. A strange blue color spread over the face of the shepherd's wife. The first stranger had offered the second what was not his to give out! She was so surprised that she couldn't speak.

"I knew it!" said the second stranger to the shepherd. "When I walked through your garden, I saw the beehives all in a row. I said to myself, 'Where there's bees, there's honey. And where there's honey, there's mead.' But such fine mead I really didn't expect!" He took another long drink from the mug.

"Glad you enjoy it!" said the shepherd warmly.

"It is very good mead," said Mrs. Fennel. Her voice was rather cool. "It is trouble enough to make. Really, I hardly think we shall make any more."

"Oh, you really must!" cried the stranger in gray. He took up the mug a third time and set it down empty. "I love mead, when it is old like this. I love it as much as I love to go to church on Sundays!"

"Ha, ha, ha!" said the man in the chimney corner.

In those bygone days, mead was made of the purest honey, four pounds to the gallon. To this was added the white of eggs, cinnamon, ginger, cloves, mace, rosemary, and yeast. After bottling and aging, it tasted very strong. But it did not taste as strong as it really was. So before long the stranger in gray began to feel all that he had drunk. He unbuttoned his vest. He threw himself back in his chair. He stretched out his legs, taking up a large space.

"Well, well, as I say," he went on, "I am going to Casterbridge. To Casterbridge I must go. I should have been almost there by this time. But the rain drove me into your home—and I'm not sorry for it."

"You don't live in Casterbridge?" said the shepherd.

"Not as yet. I mean to move there soon."

"Going to set up in trade, perhaps?" the shepherd asked.

"No, no," said the shepherd's wife. "It is easy to see that the gentleman is rich and doesn't need to work at anything."

The ash-gray stranger thought for a moment. "Rich is not quite the word for me," he said. "I do work, and I must work. And even if I only get to Casterbridge by midnight, I must begin work there at eight tomorrow morning. Yes! Warm or wet, blow or snow, my day's work tomorrow must be done."

"Poor man! Then although you seem well off, you must be worse off than we," said the shepherd's wife.

"It is the nature of my trade, men and

maidens. It is the nature of my trade. But really and truly, I must be up and off, or I won't get a room in the town." But the speaker did not move. "There is time for one more drink of friendship before I go," he added. "I'd drink to you now, my friends—if the mug were not dry."

"Certainly," said the shepherd Fennel. "I'll fill the mug again." He went away to the dark place under the stairs where the barrel stood. The shepherdess followed him.

"Why should you do this?" she said, as soon as they were alone. "He has emptied the mug once, though it held enough for ten people. Now he calls for more! We don't even know him. For my part, I don't like the look of the man at all."

"But he is in my house, my dear. And it is a wet night—and a christening. What's a cup of mead more or less? There will be plenty more next bee-burning."

"Very well. This time, then," she

answered, looking sadly at the barrel. "But what is the man's calling? And where is he from that he should come in and join us like this?"

"I don't know. I'll ask him again," the shepherd said.

Mrs. Fennel was not about to have the mug again drained dry by the stranger. This time she poured only a small cup, keeping the large one away from him. When he had swallowed down his drink, the shepherd had more questions about his trade.

The stranger did not answer right away. Then the man in the chimney-corner suddenly cried out, "Anybody may know my trade. I'm a wheel-maker."

"A very good trade for these parts," said the shepherd.

"And anybody may know mine—if they have the sense to find it out," said the stranger in gray.

"You can usually tell what a man does

by his hands," said the hedge-cutter. He looked down at his own hands. "My fingers are as full of thorns as an old pincushion is of pins."

The hands of the man in the chimney-corner moved into the shadows. He puffed on his pipe. The man at the table took up the hedge-cutter's remark. He added smartly, "True. But my trade is different. Instead of setting a mark upon me, it sets a mark upon my customers."

No one answered this strange remark. The shepherd's wife once more called for a song. But again, no one wanted to sing. The stranger at the table was warmed by the drink. He exclaimed to the company that he would sing himself. Sticking one thumb into the armhole of his vest, he waved the other hand in the air as he sang:

"Oh, my trade is the strangest one,
Simple shepherds all—

My trade is a sight to see;
For my customers I tie, and take
    them up high,
And send them to a far country!"

The room was silent when he had finished the song. The singer called out "Chorus!" But only the man in the chimney corner joined him in a deep voice:

"And sent them to a far country!"

The guests were quiet. They seemed lost in thought of a most serious kind. The shepherd stared at the ground while the shepherdess looked closely at the singer. She seemed to be trying to decide something. Was the stranger singing an old song, or was he making one up especially for them? Everyone was confused by the song, except the man in the chimney corner. He quietly said,

"Second verse, stranger." Then he puffed on his pipe.

The singer wetted his lips. Then he went on to the next verse:

> *"My tools are but common ones,*
> *Simple shepherds all—*
> *My tools are no sight to see:*
> *A little rope and a post whereon*
> *   to swing,*
> *Are tools enough for me!"*

Shepherd Fennel looked around. It was clear that the stranger was answering his questions with the song. The guests, one and all, stared with surprise. The young woman engaged to the man of 50 nearly fainted. Indeed, she might have. But finding her man too slow to catch her, she simply sat down, shaking.

"Oh, he's the—!" the people in the background said in hushed voices. They whispered the name of a frightening public officer. "He's come to do it! It is to be at Casterbridge jail tomorrow. They caught the poor clock-maker man for stealing sheep. Timothy Summers is his name. He used to live away at Shottsford, but then he had no work to do. His family was starving, so he went out and took a sheep in open daylight.

"He"—and they nodded toward the stranger of the deadly trade—"has come up from the country. They say he's come to do it because there is not enough to do in his own town. He's going to live in the cottage under the prison wall."

The stranger in gray took no notice of the whispers. Again he wetted his lips. Then it came to him that his friend in the chimney corner was the only one who joined in his song. He held out his cup towards the first visitor, who raised his own in return. They clinked their cups together. Then the singer parted his lips for a third verse. But at that moment,

another knock was heard upon the door.
This time the knock was soft.

The company seemed frightened. With
some concern, the shepherd looked
toward the door. Then, for the third time,
he said the welcoming words, "Walk in!"

The door was gently opened. Another
man stood upon the mat. He, like those
who had come before him, was a
stranger. This time it was a short, small
person with light skin and hair. He was
dressed in a nice-enough suit of clothes.

"Can you tell me the way to—?" he
began. Then, looking around the room,
his eyes lighted on the stranger in gray.
Paying no attention to the newcomer, the
second visitor burst into his third verse:

> *"Tomorrow is my working day,*
> *Simple shepherds all—*
> *Tomorrow is a working day for*
> *   me:*
> *For the farmer's sheep is killed,*
> *   and the lad who did it taken,*

*And on his soul may God have
    mercy!"*

The stranger in the chimney corner
waved his cup along with the song. His
mead splashed over the rim. Then he
repeated the last line of the song in his
deep voice:

*"And on his soul may God have
    mercy!"*

All this time the third stranger had
been standing in the doorway. The guests
looked at him. To their surprise, they
noticed that he was a picture of fear. His
knees trembled. His hand was shaking
so hard that the door latch rattled loudly.
His white lips were parted, and his eyes
were fixed on the merry man in gray in
the middle of the room. A moment later,
he turned, closed the door, and ran away.

"Who could he have been?" said the
shepherd.

The rest were silent—overcome by the strangeness of this third visitor. And they were frightened by the awfulness of the trade of the man in gray. They moved farther and farther away from that grim gentleman. They looked away from him as if he were the Prince of Darkness himself. At last they formed a big circle. An empty space of floor was left between them and him.

The room was still, though there were more than 20 people in it. Outside, nothing could be heard but the beat of the rain. Inside, there was only the steady puffing of the man in the corner who still smoked his pipe of clay.

Then the silence was suddenly broken. The distant sound of a gun shot shook the air. It came from the direction of the town.

The stranger who had sung the song jumped up.

"What does that mean?" asked several

of the guests in worried voices.

"A prisoner ran away from the jail. That's what it means."

Everyone listened. Then the sound came again. No one spoke but the man in the chimney corner. "I've often been told that they fire a gun at such times," he said quietly, "but I have never heard it happen until now."

"I wonder if it could be *my* man?" whispered the man in gray.

"Surely it is!" said the shepherd. "And surely we've seen him! It must have been that little man who looked in at the door. He shook like a leaf when he saw you. He ran when he heard your song!"

"His teeth even chattered," said the dairyman. "And the breath went out of his body."

"He ran out as if someone was shooting at him," said the hedge-cutter.

"True, his teeth did chatter. And he did run as if he'd been shot at," said the man in the chimney corner.

"I didn't notice it," said the hangman.

"We were all wondering what made him run off in such a fright," said one of the women against the wall. "And now it is explained!"

The alarm gun fired again. The company was sure they were right. The man in gray stood up. "Is there a local policeman here?" he asked. "If so, let him step forward."

The engaged man of 50 stepped out from the wall. He was shaking. His wife-to-be began to cry.

"You are sworn to uphold the law?"

"I am, sir."

"Then go after the criminal at once," said the man in gray. "Take help. Bring him back here. He can't have gone far."

"I will, sir, I will," said the policeman, unhappily.

"And the rest of you able-bodied men—"

"Able-bodied men, yes, the rest of you!" said the policeman. "Do you have some good, sharp pitchforks and shovels?"

The men prepared to give chase. In a flash, the shepherd's guests had been made to believe that they were a hunting party. Now they all felt it was their duty to go after the third stranger. Over such rough country, the fellow could not yet have gone more than a few hundred yards.

A shepherd always has plenty of lanterns. The men lighted these quickly. Then, they poured out of the door. Outside they took up sticks and pitchforks in their hands. At last they set off in a direction away from town. Luckily, the rain had let up a little.

Bothered by the noise, the child who had been christened began to wail in a room upstairs. Her sad cries came down through the floor to the ears of the women below. They jumped up and seemed glad to go and care for the baby. Thus, in the space of two or three minutes, the main room was quite empty.

But it was not so for long. The sound of footsteps had hardly died away when a man returned around the corner of the house. Peeking in at the door, he saw that no one was there and came in. It was the stranger of the chimney corner, who had gone out with the rest.

Now he helped himself to a piece of cake. He also poured out half a cup more of mead. He was still eating when another figure came in just as quietly. It was his friend in gray.

"Oh, are you here?" asked the man in gray, smiling. "I thought you had gone to help in the chase." Then he looked around for his cup of mead.

"Well, on second thought, I felt there were enough men out there without me," said the first stranger. "And such a night it is, too! Besides, it is the business of the government to take care of its criminals—not mine."

"True. So it is. And I felt as you did—

that there were enough men out there without me."

"I don't want to break my legs running over the humps and hollows of this wild country," the first stranger said.

"Nor I neither, between you and me," said the man in gray. "These shepherd people are used to it. They're simple-minded sorts, you know. They can be stirred up to anything in a moment. They'll have him ready for me before the morning, and no trouble to me at all."

"Oh, they'll have him, all right," said the first stranger. "And we shall have saved ourselves any work in the matter."

"True, true. Well, I will be off to Casterbridge now. Going the same way?"

"No, I am sorry to say! I have to get home over there." He nodded to the right.

By this time the man in gray had finished the mead in the mug. After shaking hands and wishing each other well, the two men went their own ways.

In the meantime, the shepherd and his guests were chasing the third stranger. When they found that the hangman was no longer with them, they became confused. With no plan at all, they went down the hills in several directions. Several lost their footing on the wet slope and slid sharply down. Lanterns rolled from their hands to the bottom.

The men wandered about for quite some time. Then they came together to report any news. The group found itself near a lonely ash tree. It was the only tree on this part of the downs. And here a figure was standing a little to one side of the trunk. As still as the tree-trunk itself stood the stranger they were chasing. His outline was clear against the moonlit sky. Silently, the band of men came near and faced him.

"Your money or your life!" said the policeman to the still figure.

"No, no!" whispered the dairyman. "It

isn't our side that says that. That's what criminals say. We are on the side of the law!"

Now the man under the tree seemed to notice them for the first time. He gave the men no chance to show their bravery, but walked slowly toward them. He was indeed the fair-haired little man—the third stranger. But now his fear seemed to be gone.

"Well, travelers," he said, "did I hear you speak to me?"

"You did. We are taking you as our prisoner at once!" said the policeman. "You are arrested on the charge of escaping Casterbridge jail. We know that you are to be hung tomorrow morning. Neighbors, do your duty. Take the fellow!"

On hearing the charge, the man seemed to understand. He did not say another word. Quietly he gave himself up to the search party. With their sticks in their hands, they circled him on all sides. Then they marched him back toward the shepherd's cottage.

It was eleven o'clock by the time they arrived. Light shone from the open door. The sound of men's voices came from within. It seemed that something new had happened while they were gone. As they came in the door, two officers from the Casterbridge jail were standing by the dancing fire.

"Gentlemen," said the policeman who had been at the party, "I have brought back your man. It was dangerous, indeed—but everyone must do his duty! He is right inside this circle of able-bodied persons. Men, bring forward your prisoner!" And the third stranger was led into the light.

"Who is this?" said one of the officers.

"The man who escaped," said the policeman.

"Certainly not," one officer said. The other agreed.

"But how can this be?" asked the policeman. "This man was frightened out of his wits by the sight of the hangman." Then he described the strange actions of the third stranger when he heard the hangman's song.

"I can't understand it," said the officer coolly. "All I know is that this is not the man we're after. The fellow we're looking for is quite different. He is much thinner. He has dark hair and eyes, and is rather good-looking. The man we're looking for has a deep voice. If you heard that voice once, you'd never mistake it as long as you lived."

"Why, it was the man in the chimney corner!"

"So you haven't got the man, after all?" asked the officer.

"Let me explain, sir," said the policeman who had been at the party. "He's the man we were in search of, that's true. Yet he's not the man we were in search of. The man we were looking for was not the man we wanted. Sir, do you understand? It was the man in the chimney corner!"

"A pretty kettle of fish altogether!" said the officer. "You had better start for the other man at once."

The prisoner now spoke for the first time. The talk about the man in the chimney corner seemed to have moved him. "Sir," he said, stepping forward to the officer, "take no more trouble about me. The time has come when I may as well speak. I have done nothing. The man to be hung is my brother.

"Early this afternoon I left home. I was going to Casterbridge jail to say good-by to him. Then I became lost. I stopped here to rest and ask my way. When I opened the door, I saw before me the very man that I thought to see in the Casterbridge jail. My brother was in this chimney-corner. And sitting next to him was the hangman who'd come to take his life! There he was, singing a song about hanging. He had no idea that it was his victim who was close by, joining his song.

"My brother gave me a look. I knew that it meant, 'Don't let on what you see. My life depends on it.' I was so frightened that I could hardly stand. Not knowing what I did, I turned and hurried away."

The story had the ring of truth. "And you know where your brother is now?" asked the officer.

"I do not. I have not seen him since I closed this door."

"That's true, for we have been between you ever since," said the policeman.

"Where would he run to? What is his trade?"

"He is a watch and clock maker, sir," the third traveler answered.

"He said he was a wheel-maker," said the policeman.

"The wheels of clocks and watches, he meant, no doubt," said Shepherd Fennel.

"I thought his hands were very white for his trade."

"There is no sense in keeping this poor man," said the officer. "Our business lies with the other."

And so the little man was let go. But he looked no less sad as he went on his way out. The clock struck midnight. Everyone decided that it was too late to go back to the search. The next morning, they would all go out again.

At dawn, the search for the clever sheep-stealer began once more. But now the planned punishment seemed too cruel for the crime. A great many of the country-folk had been thinking it over. Now they were on the side of the criminal. The story of his coolness and daring in making friends with the hangman had won their hearts.

Now they did not look as hard as they might have for the runaway. They searched paths and roads, but did not look in their own barns and stables. Thus the days and weeks passed with no news of the escaped man.

In the end, the deep-voiced man of the chimney corner was never captured. Some said that he went across the sea. Others said that he hid himself in a big city. At any rate, the gentleman in gray never had the chance to do his morning's work at Casterbridge. And he never again met the friend who sang and drank mead with him.

The grass has long been green on the graves of Shepherd Fennel and his thrifty wife. The guests who made up the christening party are all gone as well. The baby in whose honor they all had met is now an old woman. But the visit of the three strangers that night is as well-known as ever. In the country around Higher Crowstairs, the story is still told.

Tony Kytes, the Arch-Deceiver

Can a fellow be *too* popular for his own good? In this amusing story, a "ladies' man" gets carried away. How can he marry all three of his sweethearts? What will he say when they all get together?

"Why did you leave me for that other one? In what way is she better than I?"

Tony Kytes, the Arch-Deceiver

I shall never forget Tony's round little face. He was not a handsome man. Here and there, you could still see a mark left by smallpox. But it was not enough to hurt his looks in a woman's eye. He was very serious looking and unsmiling, that young man. It really seemed as if he never laughed at all.

The truth was that Tony Kytes looked more like a boy than a man. There was no more sign of a whisker on his face than on the palm of my hand. But he was quite the women's favorite. They liked him—and he loved them. A whole lot of them.

In the course of time, Tony settled down to one girl in particular. She was Milly Richards, a nice, light, sweet little thing. Soon they were engaged to be married. One Saturday he had been to market to do business for his father. As he was driving the wagon home that afternoon, he stopped at the foot of a hill. Who should he see waiting for him at the top but Unity Sallet! Unity was a pretty girl. She was one of the girls Tony had been seeing before he'd asked Milly to marry him.

When the wagon reached the top of the hill, the girl spoke to him. "My dear Tony, will you give me a lift home?"

"That I will, darling," said Tony. "How could I say no to you?"

Unity smiled a smile, and up she hopped. On she drove with Tony.

"Tony," she said, in a sort of pleasant, teasing way. "Why did you leave me for that other one? In what way is she better than I? I should have made you a finer wife, I'm sure. And a more loving one, too. It isn't girls that are easily won that are the best, you know. Think how long we've known each other. It's been ever since we were children almost—now hasn't it, Tony?"

"Yes, that it has," Tony said.

"And you have never found anything wrong with me, have you, Tony? Now tell me the truth."

"I never have, upon my life," Tony said.

"And, can you say I'm not pretty, Tony? Now look at me!"

He let his eyes light upon her for a long while. "I really can't," he said. "In fact, I never saw before that you were so pretty!"

"Prettier than she?" Unity asked in a teasing way.

What Tony would have said to that, nobody knows. Before he could speak, he saw something just up ahead, over a row of bushes past the turn. It was a feather he knew well—the feather in Milly's hat! It was Milly, the girl whom he had been thinking of marrying that very week.

"Unity," he said, as calm as he could, "here's Milly coming. Now I shall catch it if she sees you riding here with me. At any moment, she will be turning the corner. If you get down from the wagon, she will see you standing in the road. She'll know that we have been riding together. Now, dearest Unity, let's not have any unpleasantness. I know you don't want trouble any more than I do.

"Will you lie down in the back of the wagon and let me cover you with the blanket? Please, dear—until Milly has passed? It will all be done in a minute. Oh, do! And I'll think over what we have said. Perhaps I shall put a loving question to you after all—instead of to Milly. It isn't true that it is all settled between her and me."

Unity Sallet said yes. She lay down at the back end of the wagon, and Tony covered her over. She didn't take up much room. Indeed, the wagon seemed to be empty except for the big blanket. Then he drove on to meet Milly.

"My dear Tony!" cried Milly with a little frown on her face. "How long you have taken coming home! Don't you want to get back to Upper Longpuddle? I've come to meet you as you asked me, and to ride back with you. We can talk about our future home. Remember—you asked me to meet you. And I've come as I promised. I wouldn't have come if you hadn't asked, Mr. Tony!"

"Ay, my dear, I did ask you. To be sure, I did, now that I think of it. But I had quite forgot it. To ride back with me, did you say, dear Milly?"

"Well, of course! What else can I do? Surely you don't want me to walk, now that I've come all this way?"

"Well, of course! I was thinking you might be going on to town to meet your mother. I saw her there. She looked as if she might be waiting for you."

"Oh, no. She's home now. She came across the fields, and got back before you."

"Ah! I didn't know that," Tony said. There was no way to get around it. He had to take her up beside him.

Tony and Milly talked on very pleasantly. They looked at the trees, and beasts, and birds, and bugs. They watched the farmers at work in the fields. Pretty soon, who should Tony see at the upstairs window of a house by the side of the road? It was Hannah Jolliver, another young beauty. She was the very first woman that Tony had fallen in love with. That was before Milly and before Unity. In fact, he had almost asked Hannah to marry him instead of Milly. She was, indeed, a more beautiful girl than Milly Richards. But he had not thought much about her just lately.

"Listen, my dear Milly," said Tony, "my coming wife, as I may call you." He talked quietly so that Unity could not hear. "I see a young woman looking out of a window. I think she may call to me. The fact is, Milly, she had the idea that I was wishing to marry her. Now she has discovered that I've asked another—and a prettier lady than she. But I'm rather afraid of her anger if she sees us together. Now Milly, would you do me a favor? Please say yes, my sweet wife-to-be."

"Certainly, dearest Tony," said Milly.

"Would you crawl under the empty sacks just here in the front of the wagon? Would you hide out of sight there until we have passed the house? She hasn't seen us yet. Let us have peace and goodwill since it is almost Christmas. If you hide, there will be no ugly feelings. Surely that's the kind thing to do!"

"I don't mind. Anything to make you happy, Tony," Milly said. And so, though she didn't care much for his plan, she crawled under the sacks just behind the seat. Unity was still hidden at the other end of the wagon. Soon they drove up to the road-side house. Hannah had seen him coming. She waited at the window, looking down upon him. She tossed her head and smiled.

"Well, aren't you going to be friendly enough to ask me to ride home with you?" she said. Tony had planned to drive past with a smile and a nod.

"Ah, to be sure! What was I thinking of?" said Tony, not knowing what else to say. "But I thought you were staying at your aunt's house."

"No, I am not," she said. "Don't you see that I'm wearing my hat and jacket? I have only called to see her on my way home. How can you be so stupid, Tony?"

"In that case—ah—of course you must come along with me," Tony said. He felt the sweat rising up inside his clothes. Pulling back on his horse, he waited until she'd come downstairs. Then he helped her up beside him. He drove on again. Now his face was as worried and long as a round little face can be.

Hannah looked into his eyes. "This is nice, isn't it, Tony?" she said to him. "I like riding with you."

Then Tony looked into Hannah's eyes. "And I with you," he said after a while. In short, having seen her again, he warmed up. The more he looked at her, the more he liked her. Now he couldn't for the life of him think of anything but the girl beside him. Why had he ever said a word about marriage to Milly or Unity while Hannah Jolliver was around? So they sat a little closer until their shoulders were touching. Over and over again Tony thought about how pretty Hannah was. His words to her grew sweeter and sweeter. He called her "dear Hannah" in a whisper at last.

"You have settled it with Milly by this time, I suppose," said she.

"No, not exactly," Tony whispered.

"What? How quietly you talk, Tony."

"Yes, I have a kind of sore throat. I said, not exactly."

"I suppose you mean to?"

"Well, as to that—" His eyes rested on her face, and hers on his. He wondered how he could have been such a fool as to leave Hannah. "My sweet Hannah!" he burst out, taking her hand. He couldn't help himself. Now he had quite forgotten Milly and Unity, and all the world besides. "*Settled* it? I don't think I have!"

"What was that?" said Hannah.

"What?" said Tony, letting go of her hand.

"Surely I heard a little screaming squeak under those sacks. Why, you've been carrying corn, and there's mice in this wagon. Oh, I declare!" She pulled up the hem of her gown.

"Oh, no! It is just the squeak of the wheels," said Tony. "Sometimes they go like that in dry weather."

"Perhaps it was. Well now, be honest, dear Tony. Do you like her better than me? I may have been cold to you, but I'll tell the truth at last. I do like you, Tony. I wouldn't say no if you asked me—you know what question."

Tony was quite won over by this pretty girl. Now he remembered that she had been hard to please and that she had a stubborn way about her at times. First he peeked over his shoulder. Then he whispered very softly, "I haven't *quite* promised her. I think I can get out of it. Then I'll ask you that question that you've been wanting to hear."

"Throw over Milly? To marry me! How delightful!" broke out Hannah, quite loudly. She clapped her hands.

At this, there was a real squeak. It was a loud, angry, unhappy squeak. Then came a long moan. It was the sound of a heart breaking. The empty sacks began to move.

"Something is there!" cried Hannah.

"It's nothing, really," said Tony. He began to pray silently for a way out of this. "I didn't tell you at first, because I thought it might frighten you. But, Hannah—I have two ferrets in a bag under there, for rabbit hunting. They fight sometimes. I don't want anyone to know. It's really not fair hunting with them, you see.

"Oh, they can't get out. Don't worry. You are quite safe! And what a fine day it is, isn't it, Hannah? For this time of year? Are you going to market next Saturday? How is your aunt now?" And so Tony went on, trying to keep her from talking about love within Milly's hearing.

But he found that he had his work cut out for him. In a panic, he looked about for a way to get out of this mess. Nearing home, he saw his father in a nearby field. The old man was waving his hand as if he wished to talk to Tony.

"Would you mind holding the horses for a moment, Hannah?" he said. He handed her the reins. "I must go and find out what father wants."

Tony hurried away into the field. He was only too happy to get breathing time. He found that his father was looking at him with a serious eye.

"Come, come, Tony," said old Mr. Kytes. "This won't do, you know."

"What?" said Tony.

"Why, if you mean to marry Milly Richards—do it. And there's the end of it. But don't go driving about the country with Jolliver's daughter. That will only make people talk. I won't have such things done."

"I only asked her—that is, she asked me, for a ride home."

"She? Now if it had been Milly, it would

have been quite proper. But it doesn't look good for you and Hannah Jolliver to be going about by yourselves."

"Milly is there too, father."

"Milly? Where?"

"Under the corn sacks! Yes, that's the truth, father. I've got myself into rather a mess, I'm afraid! Unity Sallet is there, too. Yes. She's at the other end—under the blanket. All three are in that wagon. What to do with the three of them I surely don't know!

"I think the best plan is to speak out. If I talk loud and plain to *one* of them— in front of the rest—that will settle it. Oh, I know they will kick up a bit of a fuss. But that can't be helped. Now which one of them would you marry, father—if you were in my place?"

"I would pick the one who did *not* ask to ride with you."

"That was Milly, I must say. She only got on because I invited her. But Milly—"

"Then stick to Milly. She's the best. But look at that!"

His father pointed toward the wagon. "That Jolliver girl can't hold the horse in. You shouldn't have left the lines in her hands. Run now! Take the horse's head, or there will be an accident!"

Tony's horse, in spite of Hannah's pulling at the lines, had started on his way to the barn. It had been a long day out, and he was ready to get back. Without another word, Tony rushed away from his father. He ran to catch up to the horse.

Now, there was one thing that could turn Tony away from Milly quicker than anything else. That was his father's choosing her. Tony was not one to do what his father wanted. No, it could not be Milly, after all. It was too bad that he couldn't marry all three, as he longed to do. But Hannah must be the one. This he thought while running after the horse.

But strange things were happening inside the wagon.

Of course it was Milly who had screamed under the sacks. When she heard what Tony was saying, she had to let out her anger. But she never dared to show herself. She was too proud and too afraid of being laughed at. But it became harder and harder to lie quietly under the sacks.

Milly turned herself about. Then what did she see but another woman's foot and white stocking close to her head! It quite frightened her. She did not know that Unity Sallet was in the wagon too. Now she decided to get to the bottom of it. Under the blanket, like a snake, she crawled along the bed of the wagon. Then, lo and behold, she came face to face with Unity.

"Well, if this isn't something!" Milly said in an angry whisper.

"It is!" Unity cried. "Imagine seeing you hiding in a young man's wagon like this! It doesn't speak very well for either of you."

"Mind what you are saying!" answered Milly. Her voice was getting louder. "Tony and I are engaged to be married. Haven't I a right to be here? What right have you, I should like to know? What has he been promising you? A pretty lot of nonsense, I expect! But what Tony says to other women is all just wind. It's no worry of mine!"

"Don't you be too sure!" Unity cried. "He's going to have Hannah—not you, nor me either. I could hear that."

Now Hannah had been listening to these strange voices coming from under the blanket. She was so surprised that she almost fainted. But it was just then that the horse moved on. Hannah pulled the reins wildly, not knowing what she was doing. The fight between Milly and Unity got louder and louder. Hannah became so upset that she let go of the lines altogether. The horse ran on.

Finally he came to the corner where the round hill drops down to Lower Longpuddle. Then the horse turned too quickly. The wheels on one side of the wagon went up the bank. The wagon rose up sideways until it stood quite on edge. Out rolled the three maidens onto the road and into a pile. The horse looked around and stood still.

Tony ran up, frightened and out of breath. He was happy to see that none of his darlings were hurt. They had only a few scratches from the branches of the hedge. But he was rather alarmed to hear how they were going on at one another.

"Don't fight, my dears. Please don't!" he cried. Then he took off his hat to them. He would have kissed each one of them, but they were too bothered to let him. There was nothing he could do. He let them scream and sob until they were quite tired out.

"Now I'll speak out honest, because I

ought to," Tony said at last. "I've asked Hannah to be mine, and she is willing. We are going to be married next—"

Tony had not noticed Hannah's father coming up behind him. And he had not noticed that Hannah's face was beginning to bleed from the scratches. Hannah saw her father and ran to him. She started crying harder than ever.

"My daughter is *not* willing, sir!" Mr. Jolliver said in a hot, strong voice. "Be you willing, Hannah? I ask you to have spirit enough to refuse him!"

"She's true to me, that I'll swear!" said Tony, getting angry. "And so are the others—though you may think it an unusual thing."

"I have spirit, and I do refuse him!" Hannah cried. These words came rushing out partly because her father was there. But partly too, she spoke in anger because of the other girls, and because of the scratch on her face. "I was too sweet on him to see the truth. Little did I think that I was talking to such a liar, such a false deceiver!"

"What? You *won't* have me, Hannah?" Tony wailed. His jaw was hanging down like a dead man's.

"Never! I would sooner marry nobody at all!" she cried. But her heart was in her throat. The truth was that she would not have refused Tony if he asked her quietly, and her father had not been there, and her face had not been scratched. Then away she walked on her father's arm, hoping that he would ask her again.

Tony didn't know what to say next. Milly was crying her heart out. But since his father had suggested Milly, he didn't feel like choosing her himself. He turned to Unity.

"Well, Unity dear, will you be mine?" he asked.

"Take her leavings? Not I!" cried Unity. And away walked Unity Sallet too. But she did look back when she'd gone a way down the road. She wanted to see if he was following her.

At last Milly and Tony were left by themselves. She was crying in great watery streams. And Tony looked like a tree that had been struck by lightning.

"Well, Milly," he said to her. "It does seem as if we were meant to be together. I guess it's you and I, or nobody. What must be, must be, I suppose. Hey, Milly?"

"If you like, Tony. You didn't really mean what you said to them?" Milly whispered sweetly.

"Not a word of it!" declared Tony, smacking his fist on his palm.

He kissed her, and then put the wagon back on its four wheels. They got on board together, and set the wedding date for the very next Sunday. I was not able to go to their wedding, but I heard they had quite a party.

Thinking About
the Stories

The Three Strangers

1. Look back at the illustration that introduces this story. What character or characters are pictured? What is happening in the scene? What clues does the picture give you about the time and place of the story?

2. How important is the background of the story? Is weather a factor in the story? Is there a war going on or some other unusual circumstance? What influence does the background have on the characters' lives?

3. Interesting story plots often have unexpected twists and turns. What surprises did you find in this story?

Tony Kytes, the Arch-Deceiver

1. Many stories are meant to teach a lesson of some kind. Is the author trying to make a point in this story? What is it?

2. All stories fit into one or more categories. Is this story serious or funny? Would you call it an adventure, a love story, or a mystery? Is it a character study? Or is it simply a picture the author has painted of a certain time and place? Explain your thinking.

3. Suppose that this story was the first chapter in a book of many chapters. What would happen next?

Thinking About
the Book

1. Choose your favorite illustration in this book. Use this picture as a springboard to write a new story. Give the characters different names. Begin your story with something they are saying or thinking.

2. Compare the stories in this book. Which was the most interesting? Why? In what ways were they alike? In what ways different?

3. Good writers usually write about what they know best. If you wrote a story, what kind of characters would you create? What would be the setting?